Men's Guide to Being a Single Parent

Different Animal Than Women Single Parents

(You Can Learn Something Also Ladies!)

Henry Lee Thomas

Men's Guide to Being a Single Parent

Men's Guide to Being a single Parent © 2014 by Henry Lee Thomas.

All rights reserved. No part of this book may be reproduced in any form or by any electronic or mechanical means including information storage and retrieval systems without permission in writing from the author.

Cover Photo by VladGavriloff (shutterstock.com)
Other Photo from: Free Digital Photos
Cover Design by Henry Lee Thomas

Cartoons by: T. McCracken, Pond5 Inc.
Tables/Figures by Henry Lee Thomas
(MS Word Clip Art used in some illustrations)

Printed & bound in the United States of America
First Edition

ISBN-13: 978-0615990668
ISBN-10: 0615990665

Dedication

To all the fathers out there both single and otherwise as well as the women who help us.

Also, to my parents, brothers and sisters. Thanks for being there and showing me what a family should look like.

Men's Guide to Being a Single Parent

πατέρας

(Father)

A Child is Born

Love is in the air
I sense explosions and heat
A new child is born

--- by Henry Lee Thomas

Men's Guide to Being a Single Parent

παιδί
(Child)

Contents

Introduction 1
   Why The Need? 4
   How To Use This Book 7
What Does Sex Have To Do With It? 9
What Is Parenting? 15
   Style 15
   Situational 17
   Being A Role Model 19
      Part 1 of 4: Being Present 20
      Part 2 of 4: Being a Fair Disciplinarian 22
      Part 3 of 4: Being a Good Role Model 24
      Part 4 of 4: Being Understanding 26
   Don't Sweat The Small Stuff 30
Phases/State 33
   Chronology 34
      Child's Age 34
      Father's Age 36
Get The Support 41
   Family & Friends 44
   Church 45
      Healthy and Happy 46
      Faith and Spiritual Power 47

- Network of People ... 47
- Educational Framework ... 49
- School ... 50
- Community/Recreation Centers ... 52
- The Ex ... 52
- Other ... 55
- Manage ... 57
  - Communication ... 58
  - Discipline ... 60
  - Nurturing ... 63
  - Health ... 77
  - Bedtime/Sleep ... 78
  - Who's The Mother? ... 80
  - Exercise ... 83
  - Food ... 87
    - Fruits ... 88
    - Vegetables ... 89
    - Grains ... 89
    - Proteins ... 89
    - Dairy ... 90
  - Child Dating ... 91
  - School ... 95
  - Extracurricular Activities ... 97
  - Behavior Issues ... 99

Dating	105
Positives	105
Negatives	106
Who, What, When, & Where	107
Tough Questions	113
Where Do Babies Come From?	113
Why Doesn't Mommy Live With Us?	114
Other Questions	115
Final Thoughts	117
Bibliography	120
About the Author	127
Index	129

Introduction

I had been thinking about writing a book on parenting for men every since I was thrust into the single parent role several years ago. Even when I was co-parenting I noticed that most of the emphasis in the information out there was on helping women to parent.

I saw a slight void of information out there which applied specifically to men parents. Being an engineer I thought; how difficult can it be? You just follow the normal project management steps:

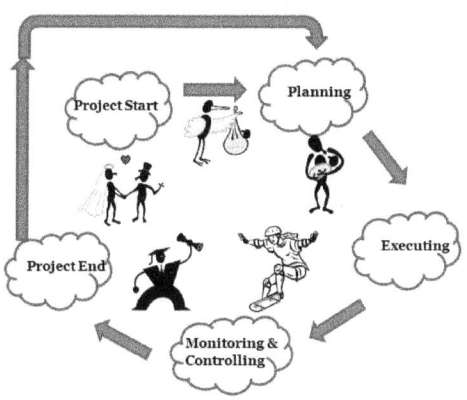

Figure 1. Child Rearing Lifecycle

Project Start

In my case this step actually started in a dimly lit bedroom with Luther Vandross singing in the background. It was planned and this was a project that was fun to start!

Planning

If you are one of those folks who did not plan on having children you will need to do some post planning to figure out how you are going to do this thing.

If you are like me where you started with help and then the help went away during the project, you will need to update your plan. It is important to plan (and re-plan) because that way you will have the highest chance of success.

Your plan should be comprehensive and include all phases of parenting including risks. Of course you would have a risk management plan to deal with all potential risks, right? If I had only included the risk of being a single parent in my plan!

Introduction

Executing

This step includes all the items you can imagine in raising a child from infancy to adulthood. It starts with getting no sleep, changing diapers (I hated this part especially), feeding, clothing, taking to school, helping with homework, playing with them, sending them to grandma's house for a break, etc.

Monitoring & Controlling

Every once and awhile you need to step back and assess how well you are doing. If they are still alive that's a good sign.

You may want to get a second or third opinion and tweak things to make the project run smoother.

Different phases of child rearing will require different parenting skills and you have to stay flexible and go with the flow.

Project End
It never ends!

Why The Need?

As I stated earlier, I could not find a lot of information out there for men who are single parents that dealt with all aspects of single parenting with emphasis on topics of special interest to men. This is more of an issue today because there has been an increase in the number of men who are single parents and I expect that trend to continue as women are more willing (or prefer) to have the man have primary responsibility for raising the children. In addition, more and more men (like me) want to play a major role in raising their children.

According to the Pew Research Center: " A record 8% of households with minor children in the United States are headed by a single father, up from just over 1% in 1960". (Livingston, 2013)

Introduction

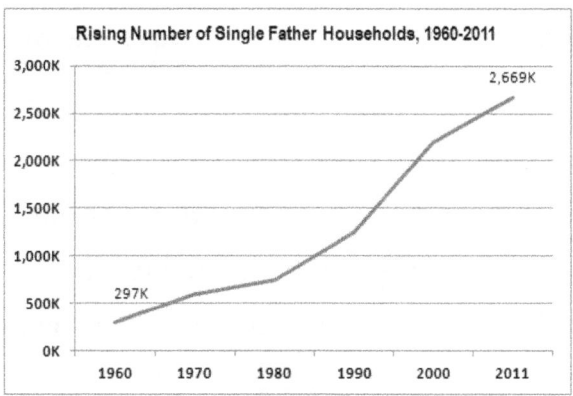

Figure 2

As can be seen from the Pew article close to 2.7 Million households were headed by single fathers by the year 2011.

Most books on parenting have a feminine slant. That may make sense since historically women have been the ones who were primarily parenting the children, even when the father was present.

Men bring a slightly different skill set to parenting so their issues may vary from those of women. Some of the big issues women have are not that big for men and vice versa.

The goal of this book is to send men down that yellow brick road of child rearing with a blueprint so that they know they are on the right track.

Though this book is geared toward single men parents (both primary and secondary custody men parents), most of it applies to men in two parent households as well. Also, many women parents can benefit from reading the book. In addition ladies, if you have husbands or boyfriends who have minor children make sure you get this book for them.

We have come a long way men, now we need to make sure we are up to the challenge!

Introduction

How To Use This Book

You may find that you want to go to a specific chapter of this book because you have a current issue that chapter deals with. Go right ahead. You can come back later for the other parts. I have tried to organize the book to make it easy for you to navigate quickly to the section you are currently interested in.

If you have time though please read this book from cover to cover so that you have a firm foundation for the task ahead.

I have also included some references so that you will have a more complete set of resources to utilize.

Sexes in Harmony

Men and Women Here

Born to Do Things Differently

Still in Harmony

---by Henry Lee Thomas

What Does Sex Have To Do With It?

Okay men, get you minds out of the gutter. I'm not talking about sex-sex. That's what got you into this situation in the first place! I am using sex here to refer to males and females.

You may ask: Why is there a need for a book dealing specifically with single men parents? I will tell you!

Men and women are different (I know you knew that part). This distinction presents different challenges for men than those experienced by women. I am generalizing but men and women bring different strengths and weaknesses to child rearing.

In her Blog, Amber Hensley lists "10 Big Differences Between Men's and Women's Brains" (Hensley, 2009).

Psychologist Tamara McClintock Greenberg also talks about the differences between men and women (Greenberg, 2012).

Robin Nixon talks about "Matters of the Brain: Why Men and Women Are So Different" (Nixon, 2012).

Jack C. Westman, M.D even goes so far to say: "Apart from the biological reality that males and females transmit different genes, there is the undeniable fact that each parent brings a different temperament, a different personality, and a different outlook to each of their children." (Jack C. Westman, 1998).

The question is: How does differences in the sexes impact how a women raises a child vs. how a man raises a child?

Women are normally more nurturing and men are normally more of a disciplinarian.

Our society (at less in the United States) assumes that women will play the major role in raising a child. This is primarily because that is how it's been in the past. Because of this women are taught many of the lessons associated with parenthood as they grow up. They are primarily the ones who are babysitters, grade school teachers, etc. They also tend to feel more pressure from society to be a good mother and to know how to take care of children.

Men on the other hand have not had the burden of caring for children as one of their major life responsibilities. Their sisters have been the ones who helped mom with the housework and caring for the younger kids. The boys helped dad with the "men's work" including working on the car, hauling things, running errands and so on; and when they got married their wife took care of the kids (even when the wife had a full time job also!).

Men now need to learn some of the skills that women have been bringing to the party in order to be a more well-rounded parent. This is certainly the case for single parent men but it is also the case for men in two parent households. We as men need to step up and have a more equal role in raising our children.

Keep in mind though that women raising boys can be bad for male children. Women can sometimes get into the trap of babying their sons and not providing enough discipline, and not making them see the consequences of their actions. Women also tend to treat their sons more like peers as oppose to children. It's as if in some ways they look to their sons as a replacement for their son's father and make excuses for them rather than hold their sons accountable for their actions. Women don't seem to have this issue when dealing with their female children. Thus guys, when raising sons, you may be able to bring more to the table than your female peers because normally men don't have any problem demanding that your sons step up to the plate.

On the other hand, men can be weak when dealing with daughters. We have a problem enacting the same kind of discipline and setting boundaries with our daughters as we do with our sons and "daddy's little girl" knows she has you in the palm of her hand!

We as men need to step up and provide more balance between how we raise our sons as opposed to how we raise our daughters.

What Does Sex Have To Do With It?

In my case I played a major role in raising my son even before becoming a single parent. I did the leg work to find his doctor, take him to his yearly physicals, had him in my home office to teach him things as soon as he could talk (I taught him to say his alphabets backwards to make sure he really knew them and he did it!), took him to swimming lessons, sports classes/games, disciplined him when necessary and so on.

One of the things I found to be an issue as a single parent was the fact that I did not have a network to assist me in my parenting. Women single parents tend to have better networks to help them with the parenting. Also there are more of them so it's easier for them to call upon their peers (both single and married woman parents) for assistance. They can take turns babysitting for each other's kids, they can compare notes, etc.

I found that there aren't a lot of single parent men out there that I could connect with and it can be problematic connecting with single or married women parents as the sex thing can get in the way. Women tend to be concerned that men may have sexual desires in mind and not just interested in connecting on parenting issues along.

What Is Parenting?

You may think that it is obvious to everyone what parenting is but believe me, many people don't have a clue! Like having sex and getting married, there isn't any required training on how to be a parent. There are also a number of conflicting theories on how it should be done.

You won't find consensus on this. You just need to study up on it and use some common sense.

Style

Diana Baumrind identified four different styles of parenting (Baumrind, 1991):

- **Authoritative**: democratic style of parenting, parents are attentive, forgiving, teach their offspring proper behavior, have a set of rules, and if child fails to follow there is punishment, if followed there is reward/reinforcement

- **Authoritarian**: strict parenting style, involves high expectations from parents but have little communication between child and parents.

Parents don't provide logical reasoning for rules and limits, and are prone to harsh punishments

- **Permissive**: parents take on the role of "friends" rather than parents, do not have any expectations of child, they allow the child to make their own decisions

- **Uninvolved/Neglectful**: parents neglect their child by putting their own life before the child's. They do provide for the child's basic needs but they show little interaction with the child.

Baumrind concluded that "the optimal parenting style was the authoritative style which combined responsiveness and "demandingness" rather than choosing one over the other". Using Baumrind's work, Robert E. Larzelere and others expanded on the above concepts in their book on authoritative parenting styles. (Robert E. Larzelere, Amanda Sheffield Morrism, Amanda W. Harrist, 2012).

You also have people like Dr. Benjamin Spock who had very strong opinions on how to raise children. His book has been updated by Dr. Robert Needlman (Spock, 2004).

Be careful with Spock though as I am not a big fan.

Situational

I feel strongly that parenting is situational, meaning you need to change your style as conditions dictate. You may very well use all four parenting styles in the same day. I think people go down a slippery slope when they think that only one parenting style is necessary.

For example, in the morning when you need to get to work you may use the **Authoritarian** style as you need to get to work and you don't have time for a lot of back and forth.

After work, weekends, and other instances where you have more time you may use the **Authoritative** style because this is the sweet spot where I believe most of your parenting should be.

When your child has had a rough time, has gone through a very structured period, or as required, you can go with the **Permissive** style. Don't spend too much time here though as it can negatively impact your parenting effectiveness.

The **Uninvolved/Neglectful** style of parenting should not be used as the preferred method in any situation. You may find though that it will happen when you are over-tasked, preoccupied, or otherwise engaged. Try to stay away from this style.

Just because I like working with numbers I recommend the following distribution for how much time you spend using each parenting style:

Parenting Style	Percentage of Time
Authoritarian	10%
Authoritative	80%
Permissive	10%
Uninvolved/Neglectful	0%

Table 1

Note that the above percentages are during normal times. Again, it's situational. At any given time these percentages can and should change as the circumstances dictate.

Being A Role Model

Guys I am sure you know that the values and attitudes that your child will grown up to have is largely a function of what they see you do and say. In addition, our values and attitudes have a way of showing themselves even when we think we have them well hidden.

Thus it is important for us to be very aware of how we carry and present ourselves when our children are in the area. This should also be an opportunity for us to do a self assessment to determine if we need to make some changes in ourselves in lieu of the fact that we are now parents.

Related to being a role model is being a good father. WikiHow lists the follow things to do to be a good father as well as to be a good role model (Edited by mico, Flickety, Ben Rubenstein, Rojo Don Poho and 84 others):

Part 1 of 4: Being Present
1. **Make time for your kids.** Your children don't care if you've just had a big promotion at your company or whether or not you own the most expensive house on the block. What they do care about is whether or not you'll be home time for dinner, if you'll take them to the baseball game on Sunday, and if you'll be around for movie night that week. If you want to be a good father, then you have to set aside time every day for your children -- or at least every week -- no matter how busy you are.

What Is Parenting?

2. **Be there for the milestones.** Though planning "daddy time" for your kids each week is a great way to strengthen your relationship, you should also try to be there for important milestones in their lives. Arrange your work schedule so that you can be there for your son's first day of school, your daughter's first ballet recital, or your son or daughter's high school graduation.
3. **Teach your children the important lessons.** You should also be present to teach your children how to complete the basic tasks of life. You can help your son use the bathroom, teach your children to brush their teeth properly, help them learn how to ride a bike, and teach them to drive when the time comes. You can also teach your sons how to shave and maintain good hygiene. Your kids will need you to learn the big life lessons as well as the small everyday tasks.
4. **Develop strong communication.** Being present for the important moments in your children's lives is very important, and so is being able to communicate with your children when you're there. You don't always have to do something exciting with your kids for them to enjoy hanging out with you -- you just have to focus on being able to communicate with them, to understand their concerns and struggles.

5. **Plan trips with your kids.** To be a good father, you should take the time to go trips with your kids -- with or without their mother. You can take a yearly fishing trip with your boys, a trip to the beach with your daughter, or even a camping trip that your kids will never forget. Whatever you do, try to make it special, memorable, and something that can be repeated at least once a year so that you've developed a fun daddy-centric routine.
6. **Make time for yourself.** Though it's important to be there for your kids, you should try to get some "me time" when you can, whether it's spending Sunday afternoon doing your own thing, or taking half an hour to run every morning or winding down with a good book every night before bed. You should put your kids' interests before your own most of the time, but don't completely neglect yourself, either.

Part 2 of 4: Being a Fair Disciplinarian

1. **Reward your children appropriately.** Being a disciplinarian isn't all about punishing your children when they've made a mistake. It's also about rewarding them when they've done something good so that they're encouraged and want to repeat the behavior. Whether they've gotten straight As, helped a younger sibling with a tough task, or were mature enough to walk away from a fight, you should let them know how proud

What Is Parenting?

you are of them, take them out to their favorite restaurant, or just do whatever you can to let them know how much you appreciate their good behavior.

2. **Punish your children appropriately.** To be a fair disciplinarian, you'll have to punish your children when they've made a mistake. This doesn't mean getting physical or psychologically cruel -- it just means letting your kids know when they've made a mistake and showing that there are consequences for their actions. Once your child is old enough to reason, he should know when he's made a mistake.

3. **Be consistent.** Being consistent is just as important as having a system of punishments and rewards. If your child is misbehaving, the consequences should be the same every time, even if it's inconvenient or you're tired or out in public. And if your child does something great, don't forget to make him feel special, no matter how tired or stressed out you are.

4. **Don't yell.** Though you may feel enraged by your children's behavior, yelling is not the solution. If you have to yell, try yelling when you're alone, in the shower, or into a pillow. But don't yell at your children, no matter how bad the urge is. You can raise your voice slightly to let them know they've

made a mistake, but if you yell or scream, they'll be afraid of you and won't want to communicate.
5. **Don't get violent.** No matter how angry you are, you should avoid hitting, hurting, or grabbing your children. This will hurt them physically *and* emotionally and will make them want to avoid you at all costs. If your children think that you may get violent, they will shut down and won't want to be around you. You should avoid being violent around your children, or around their mother, if you want to gain their respect.
6. **Be feared *and* loved.** It's important that your children know that you're a strict disciplinarian and that they can't pull a fast one on you, but it's equally important that they want your love and affection and have an amazing time bonding with you. To be a good father, you need to toe the line between enforcing tough lessons and also making your children feel loved and appreciated.

Part 3 of 4: Being a Good Role Model

1. **Lead by example.** If you want to lead by your example, then your motto should be, "Do as I say *and* as I do," so your children know you're not being hypocritical when you teach them right from wrong. If you want your children to act in a way that meets your expectations, then they should see the positive behavior from you first. Here are some ways that you can lead by example

What Is Parenting?

2. **Treat the children's mother with respect.** If you want to be a good role model, then you have to treat the children's mother with respect. If you're married to her, then you should let them see how much your love her, help her out, and enjoy her company. If you're mean to your own wife, then your children will see that it's okay to be mean to Mom or other people because Dad does it.
3. **Admit your mistakes.** You don't have to be perfect to be a good role model. In fact, it's better if you're not perfect, because then your children will see that nobody's perfect and that everybody makes mistakes. If you've made a mistake, like forgetting to pick your child up from school at the right time, or losing your temper, you should apologize and say that you know you've made a mistake.
4. **Help out around the house.** If you want your children to help out around the house, then you should help out around the house, too, no matter how all-consuming your job may be. Let them see you doing the dishes, cleaning the counters, and vacuuming the carpet, and they'll want to help out too. If they think that cleaning up is just "Mom's job," then they'll be much less likely to help out when the time comes.
5. **Earn your children's respect.** Respect is earned, not given, and you should do what you can

so that your children respect you as a father. If you're not around a lot, yell at their mother, or are only occasionally in the mood to discipline them, then they won't respect you just because you're their father. You should act in a way that is admirable, honest, and consistent so that your children see that you're a model father and a person worthy of their admiration.

6. **Shower your children with love and affection.** Though you may think being a good role model means being slightly distant but always doing the right thing, it actually means being connected enough to give your children kisses and hugs, and to let them know how much they mean to you. Don't let a day go by without saying "I love you," giving your children physical affection, and letting them know how much they mean to you.

Part 4 of 4: Being Understanding

1. **Accept that your children aren't you.** Though you may have wanted your children to keep running the family business, attend your alma mater, or be a high school soccer star like you were, you have to accept the fact that your children are their own people with their own needs and desires, and that they may not align with yours. You may think that your path is the only way to happiness, but to be a good father, you

What Is Parenting?

have to accept that your children may have a different idea of how to run their lives.

2. **Be aware of the changing times.** To be a good father, you have to understand that your children aren't growing up in the same environment that you were raised in -- even if you're raising them in the same time. With globalization, the influence of social media, and the changing politics in today's society, it's likely that your children are less sheltered than you are and are more aware of the problems and changes in today's society.

3. **Accept your children's mistakes.** If you want to be an understanding father, then you have to accept that, like you, your children aren't perfect, and that they're bound to make mistakes. Life is full of mistakes that help your children learn, and you should accept that many lessons are necessary -- whether your son gets into a minor car accident, fails a test because he didn't study, or dates the wrong woman when he should know better.

4. **Understand if your children are struggling.** If you want to be a good father, then you have to be aware of when your children are having a particularly hard time and be attentive to your needs. Maybe your little boy is struggling because you moved to a new town and he doesn't have any friends, or maybe your daughter is going through her first break-up and is emotionally wiped.

5. **Don't place unreasonable expectations on your children.** A child's life can be filled with pressures, from siblings to kids at school to teachers to coaches. Help your child understand their desires and assess their capabilities and limitations. Help them set achievable goals. Encourage them to meet their full potential but avoid living vicariously through them by expecting them to achieve what you had achieved or hoped to have achieved.
6. **Realize that a father's job is never done.** Do not assume that once your children turn 21, or they have a college degree, that your work raising them is done. Although it is important to encourage your children to become financially and emotionally independent, it is also important to let them know that you care and are always there for them and that they are valued.

[Above article excerpt provided by wikiHow, a wiki building the world's largest, highest quality how-to manual. Please edit this article and find author credits at wikiHow.com. Content on wikiHow can be shared under a Creative Commons License.].

It is very important for children to have a positive male role model in their lives.

What Is Parenting?

If you have a son, it is critical that you show him how to be a man in whatever form that takes.

No matter if he looks up to his favorite athlete, his top actor, musician, race car driver, or other celebrity; you are the most important role model he will ever interact with.

If you have a daughter, the model you set for her can form the basis of all her future relationships with men. If you want her to have high standards when she selects men to be close to, she needs to see those same high standards in you.

{ "Within the eternity of space and time, we are bound by our values, love, and, integrity" }

Figure 3

Don't Sweat The Small Stuff

I have to say that we men don't normally over-parent as much as our female counterparts, nor do we get too concerned with little issues with child rearing. If anything we or more likely to be at the other end of the spectrum of not sweating the big stuff! But we do have a little bit of sensitivity in us.

So what is the small stuff? Let's start with some of the big things (in no particular order):

- Health
- Safety
- Food
- Shelter

The above items are only big until you satisfy the essential level of need.

Table 2 shows lists of your children's needs for the four major categories of needs. For each category I have defined a "Threshold Sweat" level.

What Is Parenting?

	Health	Safety	Food	Shelter	
100	Maid	Bubble wrap	White Truffles	Castle in the Sky	
90	Personal TV	Safety suit	Blowfish	Mansion	
80	Play	Security guards	Beluga caviar	Single Family	
70	Sleep	24 Hour supervision	Wagyu Steak	Private room	
60	Exercise	Supervision	Dairy	Cooling	
50	Immunization	Guidelines	Protein	Heat	Full Sweat – Threshold Sweat
40	Healthy environment	Safety	Fruit	Windows	
30	Medical Checkups	Internet	Vegatables	Roof	
20	Dental checkups	Use Seatbelts	Whole Grains	Walls	
10	Love	Safe Products	Water	Floor	
0	Health	Safety	Food	Shelter	

Table 2. Threshold "Sweat" Levels for Child's Needs

The way to interpret this table is that you need to be concerned about the items falling below the Threshold Sweat Level (the bars). The items above the Threshold Sweat Level are nice to have but you don't need to sweat them.

Your child may want the things above the Threshold Sweat Level (you might also) but you shouldn't waste your time on these things because you have more important things to do.

You shouldn't be trying to keep up with the Jones's. If your child's friend has a TV in their bedroom don't feel as if you need to supply your child with one. Frankly it's not a good idea for them to have a TV in their bedroom anyway.

If you can do some things above the threshold without impact that's fine but it should not be your primary focus.

Bottom line is it's okay to want to give your child more but after you have satisfied their basic needs (the items below the Threshold Sweat Level) it is more important to give them good values, self confidence, making them well rounded people, and giving them the tools to become successful.

Phases/State

Parental challenges can change somewhat as different variables change. You have to be able to identify these changes and adapt your parenting style as required. To help you to figure out which parental style to use with some common states I present the below table:

		Primary Parental Styles			
		Authoritarian	Authoritative	Permissive	Uninvolved/Neglectful
Child Phase/State	Bad Grades	X	X		
	Bedtime		X		
	Dangerous Situations	X			
	Divorce		X	X	
	Dramatic Experiences		X		
	Failure		X	X	
	Good Grades			X	
	Housework	X			
	Lack of Confidence	X	X		
	Lonely			X	
	Natural Calamity	X			
	School Days	X			
	Sick	X	X		
	Success			X	
	Vacation		X	X	
	Weekends		X		

Table 3. Child Phases/States vs. Primary Parental Styles

This table is not met to be all-inclusive. Also it is just a guide to help you navigate your situational parenting style. In addition, note that when I have identified two simultaneous parental styles to use it doesn't mean that you should use each one in equal amounts. The percentages will vary with the situation.

Chronology

In addition to different phases of parenting, things can also change with the age of the child and the father. Again, this may be obvious but let's talk about a few things to consider here.

Child's Age

Clearly how you parent will change with your child's age. There are two ways to look at this.

First, the level of responsibility you demand of your child will change with age:

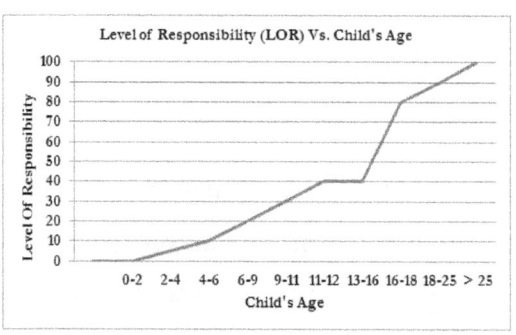

Table 4. Level of Responsibility Vs. Age

The above table shows that as the child gets older we give them more responsibility. Note that in going from age 11-12 to age 13-16 in the table I don't increase the level of responsibility. The reason for this is that during those early teen years children regress a little bit as they are trying to find themselves and exert their authority and independence. Though you will try to allow them this freedom you will have to tighten the screw a little as they unwind.

Secondly, as a child ages we need to change our mix of parenting styles. How we use the different parenting styles is related to the level of responsibility we give to our child. For completeness the below table explicitly shows the relationship between a child's age and preferred parenting styles:

	Primary Parental Styles			
Child's Age	Authoritarian	Authoritative	Permissive	Uninvolved/Neglectful
0-2	X			X
2-4	X	X	X	
4-6	X	X	X	
6-9		X	X	
9-11		X		
11-12		X		
13-16		X	X	
16-18		X	X	
18-25		X	X	
>25			X	

Table 5. Child's Age Vs. Primary Parental Styles

As was the case with the previous parental styles table, the distribution of time you spend in each parental style will vary with the situation.

Father's Age

The impact of the father's age with respect to child rearing has to do with how prepared you are from a maturity, financial, and workload perspective to tackle the job of being a single parent. If you are in your teens and a single parent heaven help you. You will need it!

At the other extreme, if you are in your seventies or eighties you will have a different set of challenges (like staying alive!).

Phases/State

The following table shows some of the advantages and disadvantages for men single parents at different age groups:

Age Group	Advantages	Disadvantages
15 - 18	- Lots of energy	- Lack of maturity - Lack of job opportunities - still a child yourself - Lack of finances - Still in school - May have to quit school - Losing out on fun things to do
18 - 24	- Lots of energy	- Lack of maturity - Lack of job opportunities - Lack of finances - May not go to college - Losing out on fun things to do
25 - 35	- Lots of energy	- Impact on job - Impact on relationships
35 - 55	- Lots of knowledge to pass on - More mature	- Difficulty finding relationships (they raised their's don't want to raise yours)
55 - 65	- Lots of knowledge to pass on - More mature - Better off financially	- No time for self
> 65	- Lots of knowledge to pass on - More mature - More time to parent	- Retiring while parenting

Single Man Parent Pluses/Minus Vs. Man's Age Group

Table 6

As you can see, being a single parent before age 18 is an uphill battle so don't do it!

It can be difficult at any age but the "sweet spot" would seem to be between the ages of 30 and 65.

This can be seen better in the following figure:

Men's Guide to Being a Single Parent

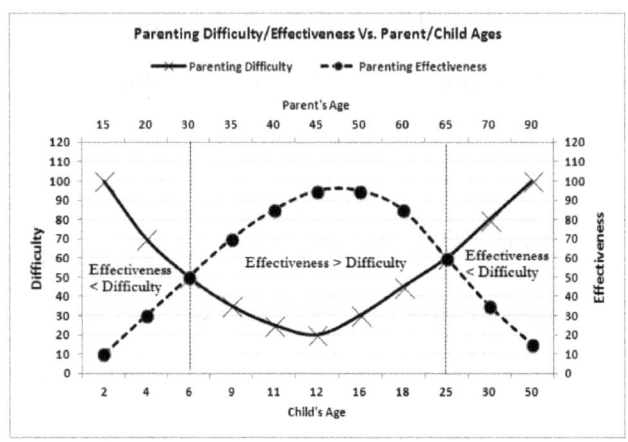

Figure 4. Men's Parenting Difficulty/Effectiveness Vs. Ages

This figure shows the parenting difficulty as a function of the child's age and the parenting effectiveness as a function of the parent's age. The data I used to generate this chart is based on my conclusions after analyzing the pros and cons of raising children at various child/parent age groups. I purposely smoothed the curves for presentation purposes given that the exact curves probably varies somewhat from what I am proposing.

As noted, the "sweet spot" for raising children is when the parent's age is between 30 and 65, and the child's age is between 6 and 25. This is represented in the above figure as the area where the parenting effectiveness curve is higher than parenting difficulty curve.

Conversely, the areas where parenting effectiveness is Less than parenting difficulty is when:

- Parent's age is between 15 and 30 while the child's age is between 2 and 6
- Parent's age is between 65 and 90 while the child's age is between 25 and 50.

Why is this you ask? Well, let's look at this.

When a child is under age 6 the demands on the parent are great as the parent has to be totally responsible for a being who can do very little if anything for themselves. The child is totally dependent on the parent at this point. A young man may not be equipped to deal with this level of responsibility. Of course at the upper levels of this parental age range (approximately parental age 20 to 30) men have the ability to parent well but their focus may be elsewhere (women, sports, partying, etc.) which can keep their effectiveness level down.

The issues are different when the parent's age is greater than 65 and the child's age is between 25 and 50. The senior parent can have many issues which makes it difficult for them to parent including physical problems, mental problems, being tired and wanting to relax, etc. On the other hand, what kid wants to be parented when they are over 25 years old? As a matter of fact, once the child approaches the high end of this age range and older they sometimes have to be the parent to their parents!

As a final note, keep in mind that the above effectiveness and difficulty curves only apply to men parents. The associated curves for women are probably very different as women tend to mature earlier than men and the differences between men and women identified earlier comes into play to produce different curves.

> Researchers do you agree with my curves?

Get The Support

Believe me guys, we need help! We can't do it along. Besides you child's mother (if she is around) you need to identify your village. If you don't have one you need to create one (or two).

Figure 5 Just because you can't see a way doesn't mean there isn't a way

Don't panic. There is help out there. First go to the gym and get a good workout. If you can't do that because you don't have anyone to look after your little one, then you really need this book!

After you get back from the gym and take a shower (you don't want to smell up your thought process), take a deep breath, have a cup of coffee (or something stronger) and relax for a minute. Once that minute is up get a piece of paper and something to write with (a crayon will do at this point).

What you want to do is write down all the situations in which being a single parent constrains what you want to do:

- Going to the gym
- Doctor's appointments
- Errands
- Working late (or working at all)
- Sleep
- Grocery shopping
- Charity work
- Etc.

Next you want to write down all the things you don't know about raising a child:

- Everything
- Changing diapers
- Medical care
- Showing love

- Being a role model
- How to feed them
- Discipline
- Nurturing
- Etc.

Finally you want to identify all the resources you have at your disposal to help with the above items (Don't say none. Give it some more thought).

At this point you want to map the above lists to the resources you have identified (by name) to get an overall picture of where your help will come from.

You will probably have to iterate this process to fill in all the blanks. If you have any female friends or relatives to help you with this process please make use of them to get a female perspective.

Remember, you will need to develop your resources and nurture them so as to keep them healthy.

"STILL HAVING PROBLEMS FINDING DAY CARE?"

Family & Friends

One of the first places you should go for help in raising you child is family and friends. Make good use of these people. Don't take them for granted though as you don't want them to feel used. You should not be trying to take advantage of their good heart and love for you. Use them sparing and when in true need.

Get The Support

You will find that your family is generally very willing to help if possible. They will probably feel sorry for you if they think you are in way over your head. The female members of your family especially should be very helpful and supportive. If you don't have any family living close by as is the case with me; their support may be mostly morale support as they will not be able to help you on a day to day basis. I use mine to run things by and get insight on things. Especially since my siblings have already raised their children, they have experience.

You will find your friends a little different than your relatives. They may not like you as much so you need to be more careful in utilizing them. If you can reciprocate support that helps.

Remember that it is better to give than to receive!

Church

If you have any spiritual beliefs you can take advantage of this network to assist in your child rearing.

Believe me when I say that there are those times when all you can do is pray.

During those times especially you need to utilize your spiritual network if you have one or get one if you don't have one.

There are four ways the church and your spiritual beliefs can help with your child rearing:

- Helps you to stay healthy and happy which makes you a better parent
- Provides faith and spiritual power which you can utilize for strength
- Provides a network of people who may be more willing to help you because helping is part of their religious charter
- Provides the educational framework to assist you in raising your child.

Healthy and Happy

There is some evidence that being religious motivates people to take care of themselves and to have a more positive outlook on life.

Dr. Steven Dowshen states that: " Recent medical studies indicate that spiritual people exhibit fewer self-destructive behaviors (suicide, smoking, and drug and alcohol abuse, for example), less stress, and a greater total life satisfaction." (Steven Dowshen, 2011). This makes sense because religion is based on faith and if you believe things will work out you are liable to be a happier person and have a brighter outlook on life. Dr. Dowshen also suggests that spiritual beliefs can enhance parenting. He lists a number of things you can do to enhance your spiritual journey and thus your parenting skills.

[© 1995- 2014 . The Nemours Foundation/KidsHealth®. Reprinted with permission.)
(http://kidshealth.org/parent/emotions/feelings/spirituality.html#)].

Faith and Spiritual Power

Enrique Colon-Baco states that "The Strength of Religious Beliefs is Important for Subjective Well-Being." (Colón-Bacó, 2010).

I have personally felt the power of religion to give me that extra juice to power on.

Network of People

If you are a member of a church you may find a number of people who are willing to help with your child rearing. The church ladies in particular are even more likely to "look at that poor man trying to raise that child my himself" and will take action to help you.

Part of the church's religious charter is to help people in need and us guys certainly fit that category.

Take the time to develop your church connection and you may find that you will get more out of it than you put in, though you are not looking for a *quid pro quo* relationship.

If you don't belong to (or choose not to belong to) a church you should consider it if you are a religious person. In either case the church will be willing to help you even if you are not a member. You may also be able to take advantage of some of the religious-based community services out there. These service groups can help you with:

- Child care
- Counseling
- Guidance
- Education
- Support groups

- Other resources and assistance

Educational Framework

If you believe that a religious foundation is important for raising a child (or if you share many of the same values) you need to think about how to educate yourself and your child to build that foundation. You don't want to do this in a willy-nilly way. The best way to accomplish this is to plan ahead and set up a framework for moving forward.

As always, I would approach this effort like a project:

- What is the deliverable/goal?
- What are the major tasks/milestones?
- What is the timing?
- What are the predecessors and successors?

To help with the above, some of the questions you need to ask yourself are:

- What religion or value proposition do I want to base my framework on?
- Do I want to home school?
- Do I want to attend church and if so, which church?

- What resources are out there that I can utilize?
- How do I integrate religion/values into each aspect of my child's life?

Just one example of a religious educational framework I have come across for Catholics is the Crossways - Religious Education Framework: *"Religious Education supporting the integration of faith, life and culture."* (Catholic Archdiocese of Adelaide).

Your particular framework needs to reflect your specific beliefs, value systems, and comfort level.

School

Your child's school has a number of resources available to help you. First of all your school-age child will be in school which helps a lot assuming you are not home schooling. More than likely you will be sending your child to an outside school if you are a single parent because how else are you going to work and bring home the bacon?

Of course, if you have the option, you will want to pick a school that your child is best suited for

Get The Support

and which satisfies most of the requirements you want in a school.

The Family Education website (Family Education Network) lists a number of school-related resources you can take advantage of. Note that this website does appear to be geared towards female parents but it has some useful information for male parents as well.

Schools understand that they don't have the luxury of only catering to your child's academic education. They know that children come to school with all the issues they have outside school so they have to have the resources to deal with the whole person. They will really like it if they see you playing a direct role in working hand-in-hand with them to make your child successful.

One useful resource for connecting parents with schools is surprisingly the Family tab on the University of Minnesota website where they want to partner with the parent for the success of the child: "*Parenting for School Success uses the latest research, providing easy-to-use tools for parents and schools to work together to help support children's learning from kindergarten through twelfth grade."* (University of Minnesota).

If you have any specific issues, concerns, or questions related to being a single parent you may find your child's school counselors, teachers, and other school personnel are ready and willing to help.

Community/Recreation Centers

Another source of child rearing support is community and recreation centers. These centers provide an outlet for children to interact with other children, play games, take various classes, etc. These centers are available in your neighborhood, city, and county.

The Ex

If you are a single parent because your Ex is deceased I am sorry for your lost. If you have in-laws around they may be more willing to help as it gives them more opportunities to spend time with their grandchildren.

If your Ex is around, getting help from her can be tricky. You may get more help than you want or none at all.

You may also get "negative help". That is to say the Ex may do more harm than good. I will discuss this later on in the "Who's the Mother" chapter.

The best case scenario is that you and your Ex are on good terms, have the child's best interest at heart, and work together to raise your child in a positive, supporting, and nurturing environment. The only difference is you and the Ex don't live together and you are not having sex together (or are you?).

If the above scenario fits your situation you got it made in the shade. Utilize the support from your Ex and carry on.

The worst case scenario is that your Ex is making life as difficult for you (and consequently your child) as possible. In this case you will be limited in getting any support here.

If your relationship with the Ex is somewhere between the best case and worse case scenarios try to make to best of it and be prepared to go with the flow (again, see my chapter on Who's the Mother for additional insight).

If you really don't have a positive female role model for your child you need to find one. It is important that your child is exposed to the female perspective. Clearly your female children need this but your sons do as well.

You are going to need that female support when your daughter has her period or she needs a bra; and exposing your son to a positive female role model will help him to respect women and in general to have better relationships with females.

Basically having both positive male and female role models goes a long way in helping to raise well-balanced children. Of course the majority of single family households are led by women so

Get The Support

there are a lot of boys who may be losing out on having a positive male role model. You are ahead of the game here though because you are that positive male role model, right?

Look to your sisters, friends, and other support areas for that positive female role model. Believe me, you won't regret it.

Other

There are a number of other support resources you can take advantage of including the boy scouts, girl scouts, coaches, the web, neighbors, and so on. Many of the resources we talked about earlier can help you to identify these other resources. Just remember that it does take a village to raise a fully  functional child so find it, use it, thank it, and be part of a village for others.

Raising Children

Caged bird can't get out

Is that how to raise a child?

The jury is out

....by Henry Lee Thomas

Manage

Okay fellas, what about the day-to-day things you have to do as a parent? These day-to-day activities define your parenting framework. that is to say that how you perform these duties dictates the end result of your parenting.

To have some structure to this process you may want to define your "Value Proposition" for raising your child.

In general, A **value proposition** is a promise of value to be delivered and a belief from the customer that value will be experienced (Wikipedia).

In your case the promise is your commitment to raise your child. The value is what you bring to the table in order to do a good job raising your child. The customer is your child. This is the rare case though where the customer doesn't know what they really need so you will be speaking for the customer!

One example of a value proposition is: ***I will raise my children in a healthy way in both body and spirit so that they grow up healthy, happy, responsible, and make a significant contribution to their community.***

I am going to cover many of the areas you need to handle as you raise your child. The combination of your value proposition and how you deal with the various things you need to do as a parent becomes your roadmap to completing this journey. Of course utilize your common sense, unique situation, and expert sources to supplement what I recommend to you here.

Communication

This is about communicating with your child. There are various styles of communicating. Claire Newton (Newton) defines five communication styles:

- Assertive

- Aggressive
- Passive-aggressive
- Submissive
- Manipulative

For my purpose I am only going to use Claire's assertive and submissive styles and throw in two of my own.

Of course the communication style you use with your child is related to the different parenting styles we have discussed but the communication styles are a little different as I display in the below table:

Parental Style	Communication Style	Communication Style Characteristics
Authoritarian	Dictatorship	The parent is king. Obey me!
Authoritative	Assertive	The healthiest and most effective style of communication - the sweet spot between being too aggressive and too passive
Permissive	Submissive	About pleasing the child and avoiding conflict.
Uninvolved/Neglectful	None	Parent ignores the child

Table 7. Parental Style Vs. Communication Style

Just as you need to spend most of your time using the authoritative style of parenting, you need to communicate mostly using the assertive style with your child.

You may use the dictatorial style of communicating with your child when they are very young in situations involving their health or safety. In addition, you may have to use this style when your teenager goes to extremes with bad behavior and attitudes.

The submissive style of communicating with your child should only be used sparingly and you should never not communicate with your child.

Discipline

Parents have varying opinions about whether to discipline their child or how to discipline them. Of course how you discipline them relates back to your parenting style as we discussed earlier.

In answer to the first question of if you should discipline them, I will go out on a limb and say unequivocally YES!

Disciplining is normally easier for us guys than it is for our female counterparts. The key for us though is to make sure that we equate the punishment with the crime.

Manage

It can be too easy for us to go overboard and doing so can be detrimental to the child. Before handing down discipline we need to consider the age of the child, the circumstances, the frequency of the infraction, and so on.

We also need to make sure that the child is aware that they have committed a crime and that they are of a responsible age to know it. For example, if a one year old enters the house covered with mud and rolls on the carpet, they can't be held accountable for their actions. Also, if you didn't tell your child not to do something and they did it, you have to ask yourself: should they have known not to do it?

To assist yourself and your child you need to set boundaries. The set of boundaries you set for your child will change with their age but the key is to have them.

These boundaries need to be age appropriate so you need to take care in setting them and once set, you need to enforce them. That doesn't mean you can't give them a break every now and then but it does mean you need to be fairly consistent so as to not send them mixed messages.

Though they won't normally admit it, children actually like boundaries because they then know what they have to work with and it shows them that you care and are paying attention.

One read for your younger child is Thomas Phelan's book on "Effective Discipline for Children 2-12" (Phelan, 2010).

There are tons of books and web pages dedicated to disciplining your child. Just be careful of the source.

For those guys out there who are reluctant to discipline their child, I say to them, Snap Out of It! Maybe you have been spending too much time at those Indulgent Parenting sit-ins.

Jump in, the waters find. Just be careful not to drown.

Nurturing

The perfect example of why us guys need some help with nurturing our children is that I initially didn't even have this section in my book!

That tells you that, as men, we sometimes forget about the touchy feely aspects of parenting and I am no exception.

It is critical that we give our children a lot of positive feedback and to make them feel safe, protected, supported, loved and generally taken care of.

Think of it as mental food they need to grow into balanced, happy, and healthy individuals.

So how do you go about nurturing your child?

I associate the broader definition of nurturing your child with Maslow's hierarchy of needs (Wikipedia).

I have modified the below pyramid to apply to children (i.e., I deleted the need for sex!):

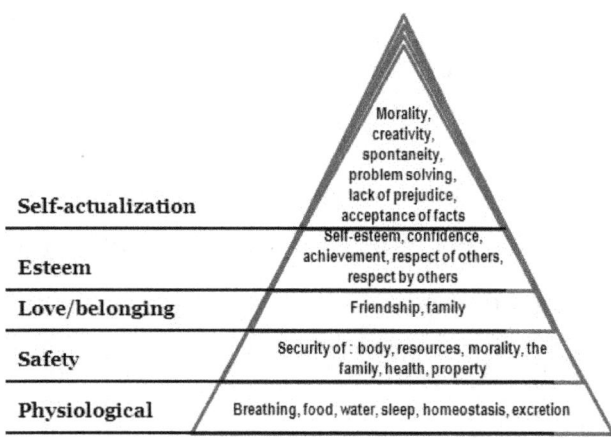

Table 8. Maskow's Hierarchy of Needs

- **Physiological** : First you need to supply them with their basic needs such as food, water, and clothing. Nothing else matters until you satisfy these needs. These are current needs in order to survive. If your child doesn't have these things he or she won't live long enough to worry about the other hierarchy of needs.

So guys, we need a roof over their heads, good air to breath (no cigarette or marijuana smells!), food on the table, heat

Manage

and air conditioning, a bed for them to sleep on, and a bathroom. "Nuff said".

- **Safety:** Then you need to make their environment as safe as possible. If your child is constantly under stress because they feel threatened it will be difficult for them to feel nurtured. Things you can do include
    - Live in as safe a neighborhood as possible
    - Lock your doors
    - Don't leave your child along longer than recommended for their age
    - Make sure they know what to do in certain circumstances such as to not open the door to strangers.
    - Child-proof your home if necessary
    - Have a medical kit for minor medical issues
    - Shovel that driveway when it snows
    - Make sure your home is safe inside and out
    - Educate them and yourself on how to response in emergencies
    - Learn CPR.

A good resource for safety information is the Safe Kids website (Safe Kids Worldwide).

- **Love/belonging:** We need to make sure our children know they are loved. They also need to have a sense of family, i.e., knowing that they belong and are protected within their family group. Loving them doesn't mean always giving them what they want or being their friends. They have enough friends. If they don't, help them to find more friends. They need you to be a parent, not a friend.

Don't expect any awards for it though and don't expect them to like you all the time (especially during those teen years). Just persevere and keep reminding yourself that they will get theirs when they have kids!

So how do you love them? First of all, tell them! Say after me, "I love You". That wasn't too hard was it? I know you think that macho men don't say I Love You but they really do and should when addressing their children. If you can tell that babe you want that you love her just so you can get into her pants you can certainly tell your children that you love them and mean it.

Secondly, you show them that you love them with your actions. Again, this doesn't mean that you give them want they want, but you do give them what they need. You also take care of them and keep them safe. You teach them right from wrong and how to protect themselves.

You do all the little things you do as a parent and that shows them that you love them.

Finally, if you tell them that you love them and give them a big hug at the same time you get an A+.

- **Esteem:** The foundation of building self esteem in your child is to love them. So you see that all these needs tie together. One builds upon the other. You take care of their physiological needs, ensure their safety, love them, and then they have all the building blocks for feeling self esteem. Against this foundation you praise their accomplishments and achievements (don't over praise them though), teach them to respect others and others will respect them, teach them to have confidence with humility, encourage them in every way; and Voilà, they have esteem.

Dr Sears provides 12 ways to help your child build self confidence which correlates with self esteem (William Sears, MD and Martha Sears, RN):

1. Practice attachment parenting
2. Improve your own self-confidence
3. Be a positive mirror
4. Play with your child
5. Address your child by name
6. Practice the carry-over principle
7. Set your child up to succeed

8. Help your child be home-wise before street-smarts
9. Lose labels
10. Monitor school influences on your child
11. Give your child responsibilities
12. Encourage children to express, not stuff, their feelings.

In addition, the Today's Parent website provides some additional ideas on building your child's self-esteem. (Rogers Media)

- **Self-actualization:** Teach your children things. Knowledge is power. The more a child knows the more empowered they become.

The morality you teach your child should be a function of your value system. Hopefully your values are consistent with what I call the universal values i.e. thy shall not kill (except to defend yourself or as required by a "just" war, etc.), respect others, etc. The best way to teach this is to walk the talk. If you exhibit high morals in the way you carry yourself your child is more likely to follow suit. You can't leave this to chance. As you are parenting your child day-to-day, when you reach those teachable moments, tell your child how morality is one of the pillars which support what you are attempting to teach them.

Teaching creativity can be a challenge because being creative implies less boundaries and structure. It requires defining an end goal with few constraints on how to get there. It can also involve coming up with a solution that is better than what we thought we wanted. Free play helps in developing creativity. Exploring the world with your child is a good exercise in creativity also.

Another way is to use brainstorming. Brainstorming involves throwing out a lot of ideas to solve a problem. During the first iteration there is no discussion as to which ideas are good or bad. That comes later. This free flow of ideas results in people throwing out all kinds of ideas, some of which seem implausible at the time. What you find is that sometimes these implausible ideas spurs more and more related ideas until the implausible becomes plausible.

Spontaneity also comes about when there are less boundaries and constraints. It requires you to be open to changes in the plan. It also requires your mind to be in constant motion so that these random ideas have a vehicle to come out of. When I am on vacation I generally create very detailed spreadsheets which show very detailed plans on things to do while on vacation. I consider these spreadsheets a starting point. You never know what may come up or what new ideas you may have on any given day, how you will feel, what new data spurs new thoughts, etc., so you need to stay flexible. When my family first saw these spreadsheets they cringed because they thought I was going to keep them on a very tight and inflexible schedule. When they realized we could deviate as we like and be spontaneous, all was well.

Problem solving can require many skills. Sometimes you need to be very methodical and sometimes you need to be creative and random. The more complex a problem is the more likely you will need to harness multiple mental toolkits in order to solve the problem. The trick here is to provide your child with the opportunities to solve a lot of problems of different sizes, complexities, and types.

You also want your child to think critically. One way to stimulate critical thinking is to use the Socratic Method:

"The Socratic Method is named after the Greek philosopher Socrates, who taught students by asking question after question, seeking to expose contradictions in the students' thoughts and ideas to then guide them to arrive at a solid, tenable conclusion. The principle underlying the Socratic Method is that students learn through the use of critical thinking, reasoning, and logic, finding holes in their own theories and then patching them up" (Fabio).

So how do you help your child problem solve using the Socratic method?

Figure 6. The Socratic Method

Well you follow the process. Say your child has a problem to solve or has to access a situation and come up with an answer. When they give you an answer you ask another relevant question which exposes a fallacy in their answer. When they answer the next question you follow through with another relevant question and so on until you child comes to the correct conclusion.

To help demonstrate this, let's give an example:

> **Father**: How are you going to get inside the house without a key?
>
> **Daughter**: I will go through the door
>
> **Father**: What if the door is locked?
>
> **Daughter**: I will go through the window
>
> **Father**: What if the window is too high
>
> **Daughter**: I will stand on a rock

Father: What if the window is locked?

Daughter: I will break it

Father: How do you keep from getting cut

Daughter: I will unlock the window and brush the glass away.

This is a simple representation of the Socratic method but I think you get the point!

To teach your child to have a lack of prejudice you need to be as free of prejudice yourself as possible. We all carry a little bit of prejudice of some type. When you can recognize it for what it is you are on your way to eliminating it. Having prejudice makes it difficult for you to reach correct logical conclusions and clouds your judgment and it does the same thing to your child.

Your child needs to be able to accept "true" facts. True facts are based on solid evidence and scientific data which are free of any type of bias. Having prejudice is one of the things which can make it difficult for your child to accept true facts.

$$\text{Optimized Child Raising} = \text{Max} \int f(S, E, L, S, P)\, ds\, de\, dl\, ds\, dp$$

S=Self-actualization, E=Esteem, L=Love
S=Safety, P=Physiological

Figure 7. Optimized Child Rearing

For you math guys out there you can see from the above equation that raising a child optimally is like a multivariate integration problem. This particular problem is NP-complete which means it's too complicated for a computer to find an optimal solution. Good thing our brains are much more advanced than computers! Frankly though, the best we can hope for is to come up with a good heuristic solution for raising our children and call it a day.

Health

Of course keeping your child healthy is one of your core responsibilities as a parent. There are many components to health, and a number of the sections I discussed earlier deal with health. Here I want to deal with some of the specific things you can do to prevent your child from getting sick and the insurance you should have in place in case your child does contract some type of illness.

First, you need to make sure that you have health insurance for your child. This includes medical, dental, and eye care. This ensures you have a team of professionals available to take care of your child when they are sick.

To be proactive you need to schedule all preventive checkups for your child:

- Annual medical physicals
- Shots as required
- Dental cleanings and checkups as recommended by the dentist.
- Annual eye exams

- Vitamins as recommended by your child's pediatrician

You also need to be on the lookout for anything that doesn't look right with your child whether skin color, a limp, etc.

If your child has any allergies or health conditions make sure that you supply them with everything they need, have emergency plans in place, and make sure everyone who interacts with your child (teachers, daycare provider, etc.) knows these things.

Bedtime/Sleep

You will get some pushback on this. Most children do not want to go to bed when they have to but it is very important for your child to get the proper about of sleep.

WebMd recommends the amount shown in the below table: (Roy Benaroch, 2012):

Child's Age	Hours of Sleep Per Day
1 - 4 Weeks	15 - 16
1 - 4 Months	14 - 15
4 - 12 Months	15
1 - 3 Years	12 - 14
3 - 6 Years	10 - 12
7 - 12 Years	10 - 11
12 - 18 Years	8 - 9

Figure 8. Recommended Hours of Sleep Based on Age

Good luck getting your child to sleep the above number of hours. If you are a working single parent like most of us are, we need to wake your children sooner than we would like and drop them off at a before school daycare so we can get to work on time. If you find it impossible for your child to sleep the recommended number of hours try to find times for them to take naps and make sure they catch up on weekends.

Now if you have issues persuading your child to go to bed or if they have difficulty going to sleep you may need to do some things to help the cause.

Parents.com provides "10 Tips for Helping Your Child Fall Asleep. (Neufeld, 2003). The reference for these tips is provided at the end of this book.

Be strong. Getting kids to go to bed is normally a little easier for us men than it is with our female peers.

Who's The Mother?

I discussed potential issues you may have with your child's mother in the support section of this book. Here I want to give you some basic tools for dealing with the problem mother. Again, if your child's mother is supportive and drama-free you have it made and you may not have a need to read this section.

For the rest of us, how do we need to operate on a day to day basis when your child's mother is not on board in a positive supportive manner.

Manage

First, set some ground rules with the child's mother. The basis for these rules is the formal court blessed support agreement which includes visitation rights. There should not be any debate relative to these items. Hopefully when drafting this document things were spelled out in enough

"ACCESS TO THE KIDS?
NO. I WANT ACCESS TO THE COMPUTER EQUIPMENT."

detail that there is no ambiguity. At the same time there should be enough flexibility to allow needed deviations. Again, the better your relationship with the Ex the easier things will be.

Try to be fair when the Ex requests a deviation from the visitation agreement. For example, if she is supposed to pick your child up on Mondays but she has a conflict on a particular Monday, switch days with her or just cover for her that day if you can. Remember, you will have similar needs at some point also.

If your relationship is not good with your Ex make sure any modifications the two of you agree to with respect to the support/visitation agreement is documented somehow such as in an  email. Also, formally repeat to the Ex what you think the two of you agreed to in order to ensure you understood each other. You want to keep things very formal when there is mistrust between the two of you. This will help to minimize any problems you may have. You also need to be respectful even if you Ex is not. Our goal is to diffuse any blowouts that may occur.

To the best of your ability you want to avoid getting into arguments with the Ex. This can be  difficult to do if she is an instigator. Remember to stay calm and attempt to work out issues in a mature fashion and to resolve the issue without escalating the situation. The overriding mandate is to raise your children with a minimum of conflict with their mother, but don't expect nirvana.

Exercise

Okay, we all know that exercise is good. But did you know that many children don't get enough exercise? The CDC found that "in 2012, about one-quarter of U.S. youth aged 12–15 years met federal physical activity guidelines of at least 60 minutes of daily moderate-to-vigorous physical activity based on self-reports of the number of days on which they engaged in 60 minutes of activities that increased their heart rate and made them breathe hard some of the time (Fakhouri THI, Hughes JP, Burt VL, et al., 2014).

"This report presents the most recent national data from 2012 on self-reported physical activity among youth aged 12-15, by sex and weight status. This report also describes the most common types of physical activities outside of school-based physical education (PE) or gym classes in which youth engage".

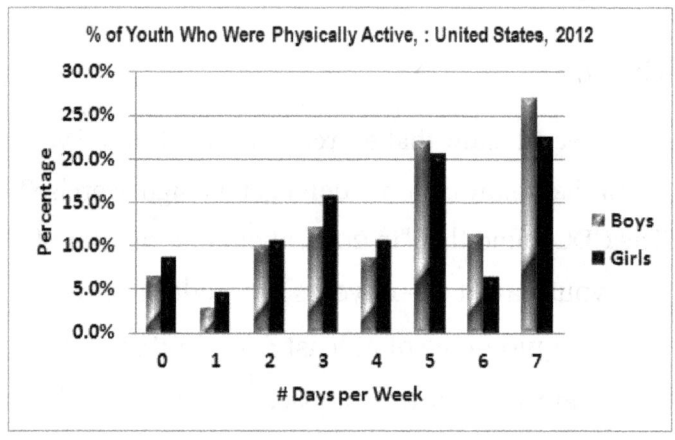

Figure 9. Percentage of youth who were physically active, by # of days per week and sex: United States, 2012

Key findings data from the combined National Health and Nutrition Examination Survey (NHANES) and the NHANES National Youth Fitness Survey, 2012:

- In 2012, about one-quarter of U.S. youth aged 12-15 years engaged in moderate-to-vigorous physical activity for at least 60 minutes daily

- Basketball was the most common activity reported among boys, followed by running, football, bike riding, and walking
- Running was the most common activity among active girls, followed by walking, basketball, dancing, and bike riding
- The percentage of male youth who were physically active for at least 60 minutes daily decreased as weight status increased.

Given this state of affairs, how do you get your child to exercise more? The Child Development Institute lists the following tips to help your child get more exercise (Child Development Institute):

1. **Lead the way** You need to set a good example. Kids, especially younger children, naturally follow their parents. So make sure you are looking after your own health and making physical activity a priority in your life.
2. **Do it together** In today's overscheduled world, we need to make sure we are spending quality time with our children. What better way than to be active together. Since kids can't be alone roaming the neighborhood, parents need to play with them.

3. **Make it fun** Put on some music and dance. Play tag. Roller blade. Basically just play. Provide them with toys and equipment that encourage them to be active while having fun. Bikes, scooters, hockey sticks and baseball bats will get your kids moving and active. For preschool children, ride on toys that get them exercising like pedal cars, big wheels and tricycles are always a great parenting decision.

4. **Cheer them on** Create positive reinforcements with encouragement and support. Help them find sports and activities that build their self esteem. Attend their sporting events and let them know you are their biggest fan whether they win or lose.

5. **Turn it off** Of course, we need to limit the time our kids watch TV and play video games. But make sure you do it in a positive way. If they are angry that you just turned off their favorite show, they might not be too excited about going out rollerblading with you. Allow screen time during designated hours, preferably after homework is done and when physical activity is finished, like in the evening or on Saturday morning when tired parents might need to catch a few extra minutes of sleep.

In my case, I had my son participating in various physical activities since he was one year old. He's had swimming, gymnastics, basketball, tennis, martial arts, and football among other things. He's been on organized teams in swimming, basketball, and football. In addition, we go on hikes and various other outdoor activities.

You need to find out what your child enjoys doing. To find that out you need to expose them to as many activities as possible and I can't stress enough that you do have to limit the amount of time they spend with electronics and watching television.

We have to get physical with these guys because they don't get enough exercise in the schools and remember that we have to set the example so Walk the Talk.

Food

We have discussed food in earlier chapters so we know our children need a healthy diet which includes food from all the major food groups but how do we get them to eat a healthy balanced diet? The earlier you start the easier it will be because that will be all they know.

The other key point is they can only eat what you have in the house so we need to minimize the amount of junk food we buy and keep your cupboard filled with the healthy stuff.

The general goal should be to feed your child healthy options from all the major food groups and to vary what you feed them by type, color, etc. The more variety there is in your food the more likely your child will be getting all the nutrients they need.

There is tons of information out there which tells you what the healthy food items are so I am not going to go over them in detail. I am just going to provide you with some short snippets to guide you along:

Fruits

Find the fruits that your child likes to eat. You do this by exposing them to a lot of different ones. Try to end up with fruits of many different colors. Note that some nutritionists say not to eat bananas or other naturally high sugar fruits but I personally don't think that should be a concern. Just try to rotate through many different fruits and keep to a balanced diet and your child will be fine.

Vegetables

So here's the tough one. Many children don't seem to like vegetables. Getting your children to eat vegetables early on goes a long way towards acceptance by your child. You will have to try harder to find a variety of vegetables that your child enjoys but make the effort. Again, variety in color is what you want to shoot for.

Grains

Whole grains guys. Stay away from the white stuff. Whole wheat, farro, brown rice, quinoa, oats, muesli, and so on is the way to go. You may not be able to avoid the refined grains altogether but try to stick with the healthy varieties as much as possible.

Proteins

Meat, poultry, fish, seafood, eggs, nuts, and seeds are your protein foods. Beans and peas also provide a good source of vegetable protein. You want to minimize the red meats and go primarily with poultry (chicken and turkey primarily), fish and seafood as your main complex protein staple. Actually in the United States we tend to eat too much protein (not necessarily the right kind) so we do what to eat it in the right amounts.

Most people need to get 10% to 35% of their day's calories from protein foods according to an article in WebMD. (Nierenberg, 2011)

Dairy

This group includes milk, cheese, and yogurt. It also includes ice cream but you want to primarily go with the no or low fat options in this food group. Of course the people in the white lab coats will tell you to eat the no fat versions such as skim milk but I say you don't have to go that far. If your child likes skim milk that's find if not go with 1% milk.

Child Dating

Okay, so your child wants to date. As Fred Sanford used to say on his television show Sanford And Son: "This Is The Big One!". Dealing with the fact that your child wants to date is certainly one of the big issues parents face. It can be humongous to a man when his daughter wants to date.

Now we are not talking about those chaperoned or group dates when your kids are under 10 years old. It's when they have the opportunity to be one-on-one with a date where sexual experimentation can occur which can really make your stomach churn. I think you have to use some common sense knowledge of your child when determining what to allow. Just remember that many a parent have been sure that their child was not having sex only to learn (or never find out) that their child was in fact having or experimenting with sex.

So what age do you need to start worrying about this?

Before I answer that question let's talk about having discussions with our kids about sex. There are those parents who feel that you should never discuss the birds and the bees with children but if you don't, believe me, their peers will and they will get a lot of misinformation. I think you do need to have age appropriate discussions about sex with your children including all the issues associated with it (sexually transmitted diseases, pregnancy, etc.).

Generally your sex discussions with your children should be in harmony with your particular values, religious beliefs and what you are comfortable with.

Having the above discussions with your children makes them better informed and can make your work easier because your children may be more likely to then make mature decisions when the question of sex comes up.

So now that you have educated your child we can talk about when they should date. Clearly that's a decision each parent will make based on their

Manage

values. You also will be setting the guidelines and boundaries with your children when they go on a date. For example, where they can go, what time they have to come home, whether they have to stay vertical the whole time, and so on.

At some point though, whether it's when your child is 12 or 18, you will have to let them go on a date. When this happens make sure you communicate clear guidelines to them. After each date you need to reevaluate the need to change the guidelines or renegotiate with them as to what they are allowed to do.

"JUST GET HER HOME BEFORE SHE EVOLVES."

Denise Witmer in her article on about.com has some "Tips On When Your Teen Starts To Date Seriously" (Witmer).

One final point. No matter want you do, your child may decide to have sex. Because of this you need to make sure they are protected health-wise. Specifically they need to get the Human Papillomavirus Vaccine (HPV). Genital HPV is the most common sexually transmitted virus in the United States and the HPV vaccine protects your child from getting it. The HPV vaccine is generally recommended for girls and boys 11 or 12 years of age. The vaccine is given as a 3-dose series as follows:

1st Dose	11 or 12 years old
2nd Dose	1 to 2 months after Dose 1
3rd Dose	6 months after Dose 1.

You need to talk to your child's doctor to get their recommendations on this. You don't want to ignore it. Additional information can be found on the CDC's website (CDC.Gov, 2013).

Manage

School

Let's be real. Many children do not like to go to school. At least in the early years all they want to do is have fun and that does not include being in school. If you are one of the lucky ones whose children enjoy school and savor every moment no need to continue reading this section. You have one less issue to deal with.

For the rest of us we need to find a way to motivate our children to do well in school. Of course you have to make school one of their top priorities. That means they have to go. It also means no play or other activities get done before they have studied and gotten their homework done. They will test you to see if you are up to the task of keeping them engaged in school but once they realize you are real they will begin to come around. Let them know that they can be focused and get their school work done in say 1 hour or they can take 5 hours but nothing else gets done until they finish. Most kids will want to get it over with so they can move on to other things. Make sure the work they do is correct and complete though as they will tend to just put anything on paper and say it's done. Remember, ***it's not done until you say it's done.***

"SO I'LL BECOME A CEO OF A DUMMY CORPORATION."

Of course you want to find ways to motivate them to want to go to school. If they say gym or recess is their favorite subject you have your work cut out for you. Discuss all the benefits of going to school including relating how going to school will help them to do the things they want to do in the future. If they say they just want to be rich or make a lot of money let them know that education will help them to achieve that goal as well.

Look for school activities which they enjoy and build upon that. You can't be lax with respect to school though. If they are on task early in their school career the easier it will be in the future.

Extracurricular Activities

It is important for your child to participate in extracurricular activities. These activities makes your child more well rounded and it exposes them to different things which they may discover they have a significant interest in. Remember that the first priority is for your child to do well in their academic courses but there should be time available to put towards extracurricular activities.

These activities are also an important consideration when you child wants to attend college. Many colleges give weight to your child's extracurricular activities as well as their GPAs.

About.com has an article on: " What Counts as an Extracurricular Activity for College Admissions?" (Grove):

- Arts
- Church activity
- Clubs
- Community activity
- Governance
- Hobbies
- Media
- Military
- Music
- Sports
- Volunteer Work and Community Service

There are many other options as well. The more you keep them engaged in positive activities, the less likely they are to get into trouble. Don't overdo it though as you don't want to burn them out.

Behavior Issues

Behavior issues in children can be very difficult to handle especially when you don't set the right foundation from the get go. What I mean by this is you need to set boundaries from the beginning and enforce them to minimize behavior issues in the future.

We have all heard about the terrible two's where children become very difficult to handle as they begin to flex their muscles. This age can especially be a problem with mothers as they tend to have more difficulty disciplining their "little babies". I remember some women telling me that it may seem easy now but I would have a hard time handling my son when he turned two. Well, that didn't happen. When they know you mean business they respond.

It isn't always easy though. Particularly when the two parents are not on the same sheet of music kids take advantage of that and behavior issues can be the result. If your Ex is doing things to make parenting more difficult you have your work cut out for you. Your Ex may be bad-mouthing you and trying to turn your children against you. If this happen don't retaliate. I know it's hard not to but read my lips: "Don't do it"! It's really a bad deal for the child when both parents are tearing each other apart and putting the child in the middle. Someone has to be the adult here and since you have no control over the Ex you have to be that adult. That's not to say that you should allow her untruths to go unanswered but if you need to defend yourself you want to do so without making a direct attack on the Ex. For instance, it the Ex accuses you of sometime that's not true you may want to say to your child that their mother may mean well but that she is mistaken in this case and explain to them why what was said is not true. Don't go into too much detail because you will lose your child and you may slip into the blame game.

In general, if you stick to that parenting style I asked you to stay in most of the time (i.e., the

Manage

Authoritative style) it will help to keep the bad behaviors at bay.

Now I talked about the terrible twos which really isn't too terrible if you stay on task. The other difficult period is those pre to early teen years. During this age range your children will really begin to flex their muscles.

With boys, when those testosterone levels begin to kick up they can be a real problem. ***Just remember that you are still the Alpha Male in your household so you just need to make sure you sons know that!***

If you have girls you could have a bigger problem because in general men have a more difficult time disciplining their daughters. If you are lucky you could end up with a girl who's a model citizen and doesn't cause you any problems. If this isn't the case for you then bring in reinforcements. This help may come from the Ex or some other female who you have confidence in to help.

Remember also that when you are dealing with behavior issues is the perfect time to utilize all those support people we talked about earlier. Take advantage of them if you need to.

For the more difficult issues you may want to bring in the services of a trained counselor. This counseling may be just for your child but in many cases the whole family needs to be a part of the counseling because the whole family is impacted when behavior issues arise. If you go this route look for recommendations from teachers, friends who have had similar issues with their child, counselor rating services, etc. to help you select the person who may best work for you and your child. If money is an issue and you have insurance you may want to select a counselor who is in-network with your insurance plan.

Your child could also have a behavior disorder such as Attention Deficit Hyperactivity Disorder (ADHD) or Oppositional Defiant Disorder (ODD). If this is the case you definitely need to seek professional help. The Psychology website lists the following disorders that may occur in children (Psychology.com):

- Anxiety Disorders
- Severe Depression
- Bipolar Disorder
- Attention-deficit/Hyperactivity Disorder
- Learning Disorders
- Conduct Disorder
- Eating Disorders
- Autism
- Schizophrenia

Now hold your horses Tonto! No need to get too excited prematurely. You don't need to immediately jump to the conclusion that your child has one of the above issues. But you do need to pay attention and if your child's behavior problems continue for several months, that can be a sign that you need to look for deeper issues.

Remember, you are not along. Every parent has to deal with some type of behavior problem with their child so there are people out there with experience and knowledge to help.

Bad Behavior

Please son don't do that

It's not a good thing to do

He did it anyway!

---by Henry Lee Thomas

Dating

To date or not to date, that is the question? "Whether 'tis Nobler in the mind to suffer"..... (Shakespeare, 1603. Copy 1). Sorry I digress.

Some people feel very strongly about this question of parent dating.

Some feel that as a single parent you should not date until your child graduates from high school because your focus should be on the child up until that point.

Others feel that you should wait a period of time (months, years, ...) before dating to allow the trauma of being a single parent to subside.

While others feel like you should jump right back into the water. "No problem man".

Positives

Okay, the obvious positive is to have sex. I would wager to say that more men than women would be happy to jump back into the sack soon after being a single parent. What's not to like?

Just having some companionship is also a big plus. Someone to talk to and have adult conversations with.

It gives you a break from parenting, though there are also other things you can do to have a break.

Having someone of the opposite sex around may be good for your child especially if your child is female as she would have someone of her own sex to talk to (particularly if her mother is not around).

If your child is hearing a lot of negative things about you from their mother, having another woman around can help offset the negatives with positives they hear from another female.

Negatives

I guess one of the potentially biggest negatives with dating as a single parent is the concern that you would be diverting needed attention away from your child. This could put you into that uninvolved/neglectful parenting style that I don't want you to be in. Having sex as an unmarried person may also be in conflict with your values or religious beliefs.

In some cases your child may resent the person you are dating (and you) because they feel that person is trying to replace their mother or replace them. This attitude could put a lot of strain on your dating relationship as well as between you and your child.

Who, What, When, & Where

If you do decide to date how do you go about doing it? Are there any special concerns about dating you need to have because you are a single parent? Who should you date? Under what circumstances should you do it? When and on what frequency should you date? What are the limitations on where you can go?

Who you date becomes more important when you date as a single parent. The women you expose your child to can impact the morals and standards which you have fought so hard to establish for your child. This means you need to step back and assess want *subliminal* message you are sending to your child with the women you date.

Figure 10

You may find though that finding the time to date is a big challenge. With work, bills, housework, and so on; along with child rearing, who has the time?

In addition, many women will not want to date a man with children because they feel you won't have enough time for them. In fact one women I was interested in dating told me point blank that: "You are a nice guy but with your child in the picture you don't have enough time for me!".

In her web article, Emily Miller lists "The Top 10 Reasons Why Women Won't Date Single Men" (Miller)

On the other hand, eHarmony lists 15 reasons why women should date a single dad! (eHarmony Staff).

Emma Johnson also puts a plug in for us by blogging on the benefits of dating single dads (Johnson, The Benefits of Dating Single Dads, 2013).

If you do have some spare time you may find that we are better off than our female counterparts as we may have a better pool to chose from. There are probably more of us dudes behaving badly than woman. With your Ex you may have just been unlucky enough to get one of the few women behaving badly!

Stay positive because there are a lot of good women out there.

The other question is when do you introduce the women you are dating to your child?

This is a tough question and the answer depends on where your child is emotionally, what type of women you would be bringing in, and how soon you feel comfortable bringing the girlfriend into your child's life.

Herding a stampede of questionable women through your door probably won't be a good thing for your child.

Figure 11

As you jump off on the dating cliff I would recommend the following:

- First make sure that your child's social calendar is full as you don't want him or her feeling left out and lonely
- You don't need to introduce your child to your casual relationships

Dating

- Talk to your child first about Dad needing to be with adults sometimes and that includes having female friends
- Let your child know that this other person is not trying to take the place of their mom
- Start your child off with group activities first where besides the girlfriend, there are other people (including kids) around and your child has something interesting to do
- Make sure you are positive with your child if your Ex is dating. You can't have it both ways. What's good for the goose.....
- Make sure you address any concerns your child may have
- and last but not least, have fun!

Questions

Who has the answers?

Decisions up in the air

What are the questions?

---by Henry Lee Thomas

Tough Questions

Where Do Babies Come From?

This question is not that tough in the early years you just recite the birds and the birds bit to your young child and they will get what they are capable of understanding at that time.

When your children get a little older whether answering this question is difficult to you depends on how open you are and your value system. This can be especially difficult for men to communicate to their daughters.

Maybe you are one of those parents who tells your kids to go ask their mother or teacher!

The bottom line is that if you don't talk about it someone else will so you may as well go for it.

So how do you go about doing it?

Well Wiki How has the answer for you (Carolyn Barratt, Teresa, Geo romero, June and 5 others). Wiki How lists the following steps:

1. Find out what, exactly, the child wants to know.
2. Familiarize yourself with child development in regards to sexuality
3. Provide answers about pregnancy that are age-appropriate.

4. Gauge the child's responses for signs of understanding and comfort

I like the above steps for addressing this question. You can read the details on these steps on the Wiki How website.

Just take your time and be calm. You don't want to traumatize your child or make them think there is something morbid about having babies.

You know your child so you are the best person to relay this information in the most appropriate way.

Why Doesn't Mommy Live With Us?

Okay so this really can be a tough one. If you are lucky, your children's mother and you got together and came up with a joint statement which basically said that you both loved them but that mom and dad needed to live apart.

Of course this is one of those times when you would get a lot of "why" questions. You would have continued on about mom and dad growing apart and just emotionally needing to be in a different place. You would have explained that the two of your were "united in being the best parents that we can be".

I was not lucky enough to have a joint statement and I am sure many of you didn't either. Even if you did you child probably received conflicting statements from your Ex after the fact.

So how do you deal with this question? First off don't put your child in the middle by putting the blame on the Ex, even if the Ex is putting the blame on you. The one exception to this is if the Ex told your child something about you which was not true you should be able to explain why what was said is not true. As I mentioned before though, try to keep your explanation on topic and resist the urge to directly attack your Ex.

The bottom line is to try and take the high road (even if doing so means you are not entirely truthful) when answering this question. Even if your Ex is a horrible person there is no need to convince your child of that and doing so damages your child.

The goal should be for your child to have a good relationship with both their parents so you need to do your part to make that happen. This doesn't mean you should try to be friends with the Ex if doing so puts you at risk or if you can't trust her. It just means that you shouldn't talk negatively about the Ex in general, or when explaining why the two of you aren't together anymore.

Other Questions

There are actually a whole slew of tough questions that children ask. One of the better lists I have found is on the Parenting website: "Answering Kids' Toughest Questions" (Spiker). You will find the reference for this website at the end of this book.

Take a look at them. Spiker cover's a boatload of questions which you may want help answering.

In general though, when having to answer tough questions try to be thoughtful, take into consideration your knowledge of your child and their age, and do the best you can. Don't sweat it too much. As long as you are trying to do the right thing you will be okay.

Final Thoughts

Here are some thoughts/lessons I am trying to teach my son. You may find them useful as lessons you want to pass on to your sons and daughters:

- Don't get derailed by being in relationships with cancerous people, especially intimate relationships. I speak from first-hand experience that your life can be destroyed by these type of people. Surround yourself with positive people who enhance you values, goals, and aspirations.
- There will be times in your life when you will need to overcome major challenges. When this happens you will appreciate all the preparation and hard work you have done to make you the strong and competent person you are. Even so, you will need to reach deep down within yourself and bring out all the power (physical, intellectual, and spiritual) that you can harness
- Plan your life so that you can accomplish all your future goals but don't forget about the present, as life can be fleeting. Enjoy the journey
- If you're a man, be a man. If you're a woman, be a women. You need to figure out what that means to you

- For your difficult problems, assess what your goal is, determine how to achieve it and take one step at a time
- Help somebody.
- Know that your family loves you no matter what. Believe it!
- Write your own book
- Having grown up poor I know that prosperity can be a state of mind. I never felt poor
- Life, economics, and impacts are way too complicated for any one theory or political party to have the totally right answer for solving tough problems. The right answer is a combination of many viewpoints
- There are some universal truths. Figure them out.

Final Thoughts

Weeds

Weeds in the garden

I spent long days in the sun

Just smell the roses

.....by Henry Lee Thomas

Bibliography

Baumrind, D. (1991). The influence of parenting style on adolescent competence and substance use. *The Journal of Early adolescence*, 56-95.

Carolyn Barratt, Teresa, Geo romero, June and 5 others. (n.d.). *How to Answer Where Do Babies Come From*. Retrieved February 25, 2014, from Wiki How: http://www.wikihow.com/Answer-Where-Do-Babies-Come-From

Catholic Archdiocese of Adelaide. (n.d.). *Crossways – Religious Education Framework*. Retrieved February 13, 2014, from Catholic Education: http://www.cesa.catholic.edu.au/religious-education/Page_3823

CDC.Gov. (2013, February 1). *Human Papillomavirus (HPV)*. Retrieved February 23, 2014, from Centers for Disease Control and Prevention: http://www.cdc.gov/hpv/

Child Development Institute. (n.d.). *5 Parenting Tips To Help Your Child Get More Exercise*. Retrieved February 20, 2014, from Child Development Info: http://childdevelopmentinfo.com/child-teen-health/parenting-children-physical-exercise

Bibliography

Colón-Bacó, E. (2010). The Strength of Religious Beliefs is Important for Subjective Well-Being. *Undergraduate Economic Review*, 6 (1), Article 11.

Edited by mico, Flickety, Ben Rubenstein, Rojo Don Poho and 84 others. (n.d.). *How to Be a Good Father*. Retrieved March 7, 2014, from WikiHow: http://www.wikihow.com/Be-a-Good-Father

eHarmony Staff. (n.d.). *15 Reasons to Date a Single Dad*. Retrieved February 14, 2014, from eHarmony: http://www.eharmony.com/dating-advice/dating-tips-women/15-reasons-to-date-a-single-dad/

Fabio, M. (n.d.). *What Is the Socratic Method?* Retrieved February 19, 2014, from About.com Law School: http://lawschool.about.com/od/lawschoolculture/a/socraticmethod.htm

Fakhouri THI, Hughes JP, Burt VL, et al. (2014). *Physical activity in U.S. youth aged 12–15 years, 2012. NCHS data brief, no 141*. Hyattsville, MD: National Center for Health.

Family Education Network. (n.d.). *Your Child's School*. Retrieved February 13, 2014, from Family Education: http://school.familyeducation.com/

Greenberg, T. M. (2012, September 16). *21st Century Aging*. Retrieved February 9, 2014, from Psyclogy Today: http://www.psychologytoday.com/blog/21st-century-aging/201209/differences-between-men-and-women

Grove, A. (n.d.). *What Counts as an Extracurricular Activity for College Admissions?* Retrieved February 23, 2014, from About.com: College Admissions: http://collegeapps.about.com/od/theartofgettingaccepted/f/what-is-an-extracurricular-activity.htm

Hendrick, B. (2011, April 14). *Most Young Kids Don't Get Enough Exercise.* Retrieved February 20, 2014, from WebMD: Children's Health: http://www.webmd.com/children/news/20110414/most-young-kids-dont-get-enough-exercise

Hensley, A. (2009, June 16). Retrieved February 9, 2014, from Master's of Healthcare: http://www.mastersofhealthcare.com/blog/2009/10-big-differences-between-mens-and-womens-brains/

Jack C. Westman, M. (1998). Growing Together: The Key To Creative Parenting. In M. Jack C. Westman (Ed.), *Parenthood in America*. Madison: University of Wisconsin-Madison General Library System.

Johnson, E. (2013, May 14). *The Benefits of Dating Single Dads.* Retrieved February 14, 2014, from Huffington Post: http://www.huffingtonpost.com/emma-johnson/dating-single-dads_b_3263215.html

Johnson, E. (2013, May 14). *The Benefits of Dating Single Dads.* Retrieved February 14, 2014, from Huffington Post: http://www.huffingtonpost.com/emma-johnson/dating-single-dads_b_3263215.html

Livingston, G. (2013). *The Rise of Single Fathers.* Retrieved January 31, 2014, from Pew Research Center: http://www.pewsocialtrends.org/2013/07/02/the-rise-of-single-fathers/

McGraw, D. P. (2005). *Family First.* Free Press.

Miller, E. (n.d.). *Top 10: Reasons Why Women Won't Date Single Dads.* Retrieved February 14, 2014, from AskMen: http://www.askmen.com/top_10/dating/top-10-reasons-why-women-wont-date-single-dads.html

Neufeld, K. (2003). *10 Tips for Helping Your Child Fall Asleep.* Retrieved February 18, 2014, from Parents: http://www.parents.com/kids/sleep/10-tips-for-helping-your-child-fall-asleep/

Newton, C. (n.d.). *The Five Communication Styles.* Retrieved February 13, 2014, from Claire Newton: http://www.clairenewton.co.za/my-articles/the-five-communication-styles.html

Nierenberg, C. (2011, February 28). *How Much Protein Do You Need?* Retrieved February 21, 2014, from WebMD: http://www.webmd.com/diet/healthy-kitchen-11/how-much-protein

Nixon, R. (2012, May 1). *Matters of the Brain: Why Men and Women Are So Different.* Retrieved February 9, 2014, from LiveScience:

http://www.livescience.com/20011-brain-cognition-gender-differences.html

Phelan, T. W. (2010). *1-2-3 Magic: Effective Discipline for Children 2–12 4th edition*. Parentmagic, Inc.

Psychology.com. (n.d.). *Child Behavior Disorders*. Retrieved February 23, 2014, from Psychology: https://www.psychology.com/resources/child_behavior.php

Robert E. Larzelere, Amanda Sheffield Morrism, Amanda W. Harrist. (2012). *Authoritative Parenting: Synthesizing Nurturance and Discipline for Optimal Child Development*. American Psychological Association (APA).

Rogers Media. (n.d.). *How to build your child's self-esteem*. Retrieved February 17, 2014, from Today's Parent: http://www.todaysparent.com/family/parenting/how-to-build-your-childs-self-esteem/

Roy Benaroch, M. (2012, February 6). *How Much Sleep Do Children Need?* Retrieved February 18, 2014, from WebMD: http://www.webmd.com/parenting/guide/sleep-children

Safe Kids Worldwide. (n.d.). *Safe Kids Worldwide*. Retrieved February 17, 2014, from Safe Kids: http://www.safekids.org/

Bibliography

Shakespeare, W. (1603. Copy 1). *Hamlet [The "First Quarto"] The Shakespeare Quartos Archives.* Huntington Library, image 17.

Spiker, T. (n.d.). *Answering Kids' Toughest Questions.* Retrieved February 25, 2014, from Parenting: http://www.parenting.com/article/answering-kids-toughest-questions?page=0,1

Spock, D. B. (2004). *Dr. Spock's Baby and Child Care: 8th Edition.* Gallery Books.

Steven Dowshen, M. (2011, August). *How Can Spirituality Affect Your Family's Health?* Retrieved February 13, 2014, from Kids Health: http://kidshealth.org/parent/emotions/feelings/spirituality.html#

University of Minnesota. (n.d.). *Partnering for School Success.* Retrieved February 15, 2014, from University of Minnesota Extension: http://www.extension.umn.edu/family/partnering-for-school-success/

Wikipedia. (n.d.). *Maslow's hierarchy of needs.* Retrieved February 15, 2014, from Wikipedia, the Free Encyclopedia: http://en.wikipedia.org/wiki/Maslow%27s_hierarchy_of_needs

Wikipedia. (n.d.). *Value proposition.* Retrieved February 20, 2014, from Wikipedia, the free

encyclopedia:
http://en.wikipedia.org/wiki/Value_proposition

William Sears, MD and Martha Sears, RN. (n.d.). *12 Ways to Help Your Child Build Self-Confidence*. Retrieved February 17, 2014, from Ask Dr Sears: http://www.askdrsears.com/topics/parenting/child-rearing-and-development/12-ways-help-your-child-build-self-confidence

Witmer, D. (n.d.). *Tips On When Your Teen Starts To Date Seriously*. Retrieved February 23, 2014, from About.com: Parenting Teens: http://parentingteens.about.com/cs/teenssex/a/dating_1_teens.htm

About the Author

Henry Lee Thomas is the single parent of a young son. He has been a single parent for several years. During the early part of his son's life, even though he was not a single parent, he played a major role in his son's life by managing most of his son's development including enrolling his son in various activities taking him to doctor's appointments, and teaching him. He has also parented a teenage stepdaughter.

He has a B.A. degree in Mathematics from Oberlin College in Oberlin, OH and a M.S. degree in Operations Research from the University of Iowa in Iowa City, IA.

By profession he is a Project Engineer with a broad interest in many subjects. He is a middle child from a large family (one of seven) and he has a non-ending thirst for knowledge.

This background, along with his introspective way of thinking allows him to analyze this thing called parenting from a unique perspective.

He currently lives in Northern Virginia with his son.

Phases

Exist in one plane

Transcend to new dimension

Here I are again

---by Henry Lee Thomas

Index

A

ADHD, 102
Age, 34, 36
Alpha Male, 101
Attention Deficit Hyperactivity Disorder. See ADHD
Authoritarian, 15, 17, 18
Authoritative, 15, 17, 18, 101

B

Being a Fair Disciplinarian, 22
Being a Good Role Model, 24
Being Present, 20
Being Understanding, 26
Brainstorming, 70

C

CDC, 83, 94

D

differences
 between men and women, 9, 10, 40
discipline, 12, 26, 60, 61, 62
Dr. Benjamin Spock, 16

E

educational framework, 46, 50
effectiveness
 parenting, 38, 39, 40
Esteem, 67
Executing, 3

F

farro, 89

H

Haikus
 A Child is Born, v
 Bad Behavior, 104
 Phases, 128
 Questions, 112
 Raising Children, 56
 Sexes in Harmony, 8
 Weeds, 119
HPV, 94
Human *Papillomavirus* Vaccine. *See* HPV

L

Love/belonging, 66

M

Monitoring & Controlling, 3

multivariate integration problem, 76

N

network, 13, 45, 46, 102
NP-complete, 76
nurturing, 10, 53, 63

O

ODD, 102
Oppositional Defiant Disorder. *See* ODD

P

parental style, 33, 36
parenting style, 15, 16, 17, 18, 33, 60, 100, 106
Permissive, 16, 17, 18
Pew Research Center, 4
Physiological, 64
Planning, 2
prejudice, 75, 76
Problem solving, 72
Project, 2, 3, 127
project management, 1

Q

quinoa, 89

R

religion, 47, 49, 50
religious foundation, 49
resources, 7, 43, 49, 50, 51, 55

Reward, 22
role model, 20, 25, 26, 28, 29, 43, 54, 55
Role Model, 19

S

Safety, 65
Self-actualization, 69
sex, 9, 14, 15, 53, 63, 91, 92, 94, 105, 106
situational, 17, 18, 33
skill set
  Men, 5
Socratic Method, 72
sweet spot, 17, 37, 39

T

Threshold Sweat, 30, 31, 32

U

Uninvolved/Neglectful, 16, 18
universal values, 69

V

Value Proposition, 57
village, 41, 55

W

women
  raising boys, iii, 1, 4, 5, 6, 9, 10, 11, 14, 40, 54, 99, 105, 108, 109, 110, 117

Index

www.ingramcontent.com/pod-product-compliance
Lightning Source LLC
Chambersburg PA
CBHW071701040426
42446CB00011B/1864